Love, Alice

Marie Elizabeth Randall Chandler

Alice Margaret Randall Cocca

Love, Alice

iUniverse books may be ordered through booksellers or by contacting:

iUniverse
1663 Liberty Drive
Bloomington, IN 47403
www.iuniverse.com
1-800-Authors (1-800-288-4677)

Because of the dynamic nature of the Internet, any web addresses or links contained in this book may have changed since publication and may no longer be valid. The views expressed in this work are solely those of the author and do not necessarily reflect the views of the publisher, and the publisher hereby disclaims any responsibility for them.

Any people depicted in stock imagery provided by Getty Images are models, and such images are being used for illustrative purposes only.
Certain stock imagery © Getty Images.

NLT
Scripture quotations marked NLT are taken from the Holy Bible, New Living Translation, copyright © 1996, 2004, 2007. Used by permission of Tyndale House Publishers, Inc. Carol Stream, Illinois 60188. All rights reserved. Website

ESV
Unless otherwise indicated, all scripture quotations are from The Holy Bible, English Standard Version® (ESV®). Copyright ©2001 by Crossway Bibles, a division of Good News Publishers. Used by permission. All rights reserved.

ISBN: 978-1-6632-0366-3 (sc)
ISBN: 978-1-6632-0367-0 (hc)
ISBN: 978-1-6632-0368-7 (e)

Library of Congress Control Number: 2020911938

Print information available on the last page.

iUniverse rev. date: 07/27/2020

Also By Marie Elizabeth Randall Chandler

I No Longer Dance

Running the Road to Galilee Book One

Running the Road to Galilee Book Two

Running the Road to Galilee Book Three

My Mother's Keeper

Rhapsodic Love

The Sick World of Sin

In memory of Alice, my dear twin sister,

living now with God.

First to see the Savior's face, first to live in His place.

A special thank you to Betty, the ever-mindful original keeper of this tender collection.

Preface

Poems penned by my dear twin, hidden away for decades too
many, now on this day I hold them in my hand.
Tears flow before I finish even just one line, knowing these are the
words from my sister's heart, many long years ago.
I feel each one inside this soul of mine, speaking to me as I read each one.
Surely it was the Lord who gave them to me, for it seems to be this the Lord is saying to me:
Here are your dear twin's thoughts, words I helped her pen long years ago.
And if she could write a note to go along with these poems of hers, it would say:

I love you my dear twin, Marie.
From the womb we shared and until the day I died, and now
too, in Heaven above, I love you even the more.
So here to you I give each poem, knowing you shall cherish all words here.
Sealed with a kiss, love letters to you, signing them now with pen in hand,
Love, Alice

Our lives are a Christ-like fragrance rising up to God.

2 Corinthians 2:15 (NLT)

In the Vast

Are You out there?
Somewhere amidst the stars.
High in stature
Low in penitence.

Can You see me?
Find me in the light of day.
Love me in the beauty of night.

Will You be there?
Here, in my life.
Comfort me in the Presence of God.

He is there - out here. I see Him at night.
Listen to the wise words emitting faithfully from His Word.
Are You out there?
Find me. Love me. Together. We.

Fall

Asleep throughout the night, eyes were shut throughout the glory.

From Heaven's skies who sent whispers so cold to cool this hot, seething earth.

Dreaming of nothing, how could I be so placid, so passive to it all?

From the Hand above who sent cooler winds to calm, to pacify, to redeem this worldly place.

Awakened! With eyes open wide, I stare in amazement at the clean, clear skies above me, out from my window.

Opened the door
and suddenly with glee
felt the coolness from rushing winds
lift my feet,
open my arms,
as I captured
the glory
of the
changing season.

God's Reign

Your chance to grow nears
each time God's rain replenishes
the lost nutrients burned by the sun's heat.

The puddles are left to be washed away
Drifting down the curbs of our street,
While the young ones wade in the coolness
squishing the mud between their playful toes.

Slowly but surely the water travels down
those dark corridors.
I watch it disappear before my eyes.
If only with a bucket or two,
I could perhaps return it to a nearby lake to stay,
in safety before the next storm.

No one can put a stop to the calls of nature.
Rain will fall, sun will shine,
each in their own due time.
I do wish I could save what I could
But God reigns over me
I will let His hand save
instead.

Feet Forward

For all we do,
words we speak,
music we hear,
sunsets we see,
there are those lives
we must touch.

Through love we learn
to bear life's burdens.
God has given
these senses in hopes
we can live
spiritually with Him.

Roads before us stretch,
Miles and miles of rocky roads.
On every path
We shall use our heart,
our mind, eyes and ears
to savor these.
Knowing all along
God is leading the way.
He has been the leader all along.
Feet forward. Live fully.

Earth's Walking

Get closer
Kneel down
Nose to the ground
Eyes open
Smell the salt
in the earth's ground,
richly scented
sparkling with dew,
dropping from Heaven.

Get closer to the One who made it all.
Creation, man and beast of the water, earth and air.

Get closer with God, the Creator,
who sent Jesus to walk this earth.
Kneel with nose to the ground.
Kneel down to Jesus.

Born Again

I've got Jesus down deep in my soul. I don't need hot or cold.
I've got love growing, budding in my heart. I don't need fast or slow.
I've got power crushing Satan each day in my life. I don't need high or low.
All the drugs are gone, far, far away. Too lost to ever be found again.

Jesus was found along the way.
Now, I'm born again!

Swim, Swim

Up high, blue skies shine down.
Through cloudy, murky, muddy water.
Strong sun beams reflect off the white cement.
Yet, the water remains cloudy, ugly to the eye.
Why the loss of blue, crisp, clear water?

Jesus can change the color.
Jesus took the dark ugliness from my life, changed it to a crisp, clear, clean sparkling life!
Praise God!

Before the Lord

So small.
So tiny am I.
A child
in the Master's Hand.

So powerful.
So mighty is my
Heavenly Father
in my weakness.

The power of prayer
draws deep from my soul.
Jesus' Holy Spirit makes me holy
before the Lord, in His eyes.

Yet I so fragile and weak,
bow down before You with open arms
and weeping eyes.
I have felt the power, the gracious love,
flow and flow
from the Master's Hand.

In Prayer

When You do the things You do, I cringe in
utter amazement because when you
DO, things are DONE.
In all my worthless ways, You continue to stay.
My walk weakens, yet still You guide my way.

I close my eyes thanking You for what You do.
I feel Your love from Heaven above.
Released from my closed eyes are tears of joy from You my Lord.
I know my life is in good hands, good care.
My life is best during the times I spend in prayer.

Holy Spirit

And now the Holy Spirit sings, rejoices in my heart.
Slowly, peacefully, in one accord, the Spirit sings songs of joy.

To Jesus we all are thankful, for love so true.
When I celebrate the Holy Spirit, Jesus, I become closer to You.

Happy Child

The happy child is jumping in my heart,
up and down, up and down.
Gaily living each day,
hoping to one day
Suddenly jump out!

The glee I feel, the long smile
is bountiful and plentiful
enough to give to everyone!

The happy child, the young, playful girl
Sings with gladness to all those
awaiting proof of God's incomprehensible love!

Closing

I thank the Lord for this tender collection in which He allowed me a glimpse
into my sister's heart, seeing now how much she loved You.
Though the collection humble, it certainly speaks more.
Her affection for Jesus surely met with vibrant joy, richly resplendent, abounding
in a passionate love; this is the life my sister enjoyed with You.

Though her life here on earth was ever so short, she lived life out loud, with the intensity and
enthusiasm found only in those thriving in the Presence of the Holy God, a happy child of His.
Now in Heaven above, her love for You is brought to its fullest, rich in a
never-ending melody, in love with God, a celebration of the sister I always knew.

Two hearts formed together.
Bound as one in one womb.
Forever together we shall spend eternity.

About the Authors

Twin sisters Alice and Marie were born and raised in Texas.
With a deep passion for writing, Alice pursued creative writing studies in
school as a teen and young adult. She was a published writer in the literary arts
magazine, Gulf Breeze, of the Gulf Coast Intercollegiate Conference.
Tragically, at age forty her life ended.
Thus, her passion never igniting to its fullest potential.
Marie's love for writing blossomed much later in life, unfolding as a
skillful writer after whole-heartedly devoting her life to God.

Having lived a wonderful childhood, spending all days together, enjoying one another's
company as the wonderful sisters they were, remaining the best of friends throughout their
years, supporting and loving one another with a special connection that only they knew.
A bond formed in the womb, rising to Heaven above.
A love so strong that not even the finality of death could it be removed, yet only grow deeper.
For it is through the Lord this love is brought to its fullest capacity.
Never swaying, remaining always.

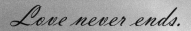

Love never ends.

1 Corinthians 13:8 (ESV)

Printed in the United States
By Bookmasters